ideal
school supply

S0-AAD-247

FUNtastic
FR⊕GS™

Making Graphs

By Jill Osofsky

Contents

Published by Ideal School Supply
an imprint of

**McGraw-Hill
Children's Publishing**

McGraw-Hill
Children's Publishing

A Division of The **McGraw·Hill** Companies

Published by Ideal School Supply
An imprint of McGraw-Hill Children's Publishing
Copyright © 2000 McGraw-Hill Children's Publishing

Cover Concept and Page Design: Sara Mordecai
Cover Illustration: Kristin Mallory
Text Illustrations: Jim Connolly

Send all inquiries to:
McGraw-Hill Children's Publishing
3195 Wilson Drive NW
Grand Rapids, MI 49544

Funtastic Frogs™: Making Graphs, Grades K–2
ISBN: 1-56451-321-1

2 3 4 5 6 7 8 9 05 04 03 02 01

This book is one in a series of books designed to develop children's mathematical thinking. Each book supports the use of Funtastic Frog™ Counters in activities that teach key mathematical concepts.

Funtastic Frog™ Counters are available from Ideal School Supply in six different colors and in three different sizes (3g, 6g, and 12g). A unique lacing feature allows children to use the frogs in a wide range of counting and patterning activities.

In *Funtastic Frogs™: Making Graphs, Grades K-2,* children use the frog counters to:
• sort and classify objects by color and size
• graph data using objects
• graph data using symbols
• analyze graphs to compare quantities

The activities in this book are designed to help children learn how to graph data using objects, pictures, and symbols in a way that shows information clearly. The children are actively involved using the frog counters to make the graphs. They sort, classify, and graph the frog counters and talk about what the graph is about in a way that makes sense to them. They use the information in the graphs to compare quantities. The activities in this book support current mathematics standards.

Contents
This book contains 22 activities divided into sections. Each section contains similar activities, giving children the opportunity to apply and practice each skill.

Sample solutions are provided on page 7. A photocopy master for the frog counters is also included on page 8. Photocopy masters for two sizes of graphing paper are included on pages 9 and 10.

Math Skills and Understandings	Related Activities
Sort and classify objects	Activities 1-22
Collect and represent data	Activities 1-22
Use concrete objects to represent data	Activities 1-22
Display data using sorting diagrams	Activities 1-4
Display data using graphs	Activities 5-22
Analyze graphs to compare quantities	Activities 7-22

Suggestions for Classroom Use

The activities are sequenced by level of difficulty within each section and from section to section. Modify a section if you find it is too challenging for your children, or not challenging enough.

The activities can be introduced to the whole group using an overhead projector, the chalkboard, or sitting in a circle on the floor. The first several activities should be done with the whole group to model the graphing process. Once several activities have been done as a group and children understand the directions, they can work in pairs, small groups, or individually at a learning center to complete each activity.

Encourage children to share their thinking with the whole class. Talking about their thinking helps them clarify their thoughts and allows others to hear how they might solve the same problem a different way. Talking about how they solve problems helps children make mathematical connections and deepens their understanding.

Materials

You may wish to make an overhead transparency of the first activity page for each section as an introduction to the activities that follow.

For each pupil, pair of children, or group, you will need:
- pencils
- crayons or colored markers to match the colors of the frog counters
- a tub of small and medium frog counters in six colors
- an activity page for each child

Introducing the Activities

Before beginning the activities in this book, it is important to allow time for children to freely explore the frog counters. This will allow them to satisfy their curiosity about the frogs before using them in the activities. Encourage the children to compare the frogs and tell how they are alike and how they are different. Then have them find different ways to sort or group the frogs. Ask them to describe the sizes and weights.

This exploration prior to beginning the activities provides an opportunity to introduce vocabulary used throughout the book. Introduce terms such as *sort, collect, represent, diagram, graph,* and *set* informally. Use the terms that are appropriate for your children's age level. It is also a good time to introduce the symbols that will appear on some activity pages. The frog sizes are referred to as *small* and *medium*. The color for each frog is represented by the first letter of each color on the chest of the frog. Be sure all pupils are familiar with these terms before you begin instruction.

When you introduce a section of the book, lead the children through the first few activities in that section. Point out the need for a title, a label for the axis, and numbers on each graph. It is important that the whole class participate in making model graphs before constructing graphs in small groups. Discuss the directions and how to record their work.

Once a graph is completed, the most important activity is discussing what the graph represents. When reviewing an activity with the group, encourage the children to talk about their discoveries. Ask such questions as: *What does this graph tell us? Which row (column) has more (fewer) frogs? How many more (fewer)?* Talking about the graphs will help the children make connections between the making of the graph and the information it represents.

Mathematical Content by Section

Activities 1-4: Sorting by color and size. Use Activity 1 as an introduction to Activities 2-6. Have the children match the frogs and sort them by color, then sort them by size. Skills required making a graph include sorting and classifying. The activity pages review these skills.

Activities 5-6: Graphing color and size. Children sort frog counters by colors and sizes then graph, count, and compare the data. The vertical graphs in each activity begin at the bottom of the page and are built up. These activities provide children with a model of how to organize a graph. Point out the need for a title, a label for the axis, and numbers on the graph. Discuss each graph as a group, asking such questions as: *How many green frogs? Which group has more frogs? How many more?*

Activities 7-14: Organizing data using vertical graphs. Use Activity 7, Frog Pond, as an introduction to Activities 8-10. Have the children match the frogs then sort them by color. Use Activity 11, Frog Park, as an introduction to Activities 12-14. Have the children match the frogs then sort them by color. In Activities 8-14 children place frogs on the graphs to represent the data. Children color squares in the graph to record, then compare the number of frogs and discuss what the graphs represent.

Activities 15-22: Organizing data using horizontal graphs. Use Activity 15, Frog House, as an introduction to Activities 16-18. Have the children match the frogs then sort them by size and color. Use Activity 19, Frog Town, in the same way as introduction to Activities 20-22. The graphs in these activities are presented in a horizontal format so children learn that a graph can be constructed in more than one way. In Activities 16-22 children place frogs on the graphs to represent the data. They color squares in the graphs to record, then compare the number of frogs and discuss what the graphs represent.

Sample Solutions

These are sample solutions. Additional solutions are possible for some activities.

Activity

1A 3 green frogs
1B 4 blue frogs

2A 5 small frogs
2B 3 medium frogs
2C medium frogs
2D 2

3A 6 small yellow frogs
3B 3 medium red frogs
3C small yellow frogs
3D 3

4A 6 small purple frogs
4B 2 medium orange frogs
4C small purple frogs
4D 4

5A 2 small yellow frogs
5B 4 small orange frogs
5C orange frogs
5D 2

6A 5 red frogs
6B 1 blue frog
6C blue frogs
6D 4

8A 5 green frogs
8B 3 yellow frogs
8C green frogs
8D 2

9A 2 red frogs
9B 4 blue frogs
9C red frogs
9D 2

10A 2 orange frogs
10B 5 purple frogs
10C purple frogs
10D 3

12A 5 green frogs
12B 4 yellow frogs
12C 3 orange frogs
12D green frogs
12E orange frogs

Activity

13A 3 orange frogs
13B 4 purple frogs
13C 2 blue frogs
13D purple frogs
13E blue frogs

14A 2 blue frogs
14B 5 green frogs
14C 4 purple frogs
14D green frogs
14E blue frogs

16A 5 small yellow frogs
16B 4 medium orange frogs
16C small yellow frogs
16D 1

17A 5 small green frogs
17B 3 small purple frogs
17C 4 medium orange frogs
17D small green frogs
17E small purple frogs

18A 5 small yellow frogs
18B 1 small blue frog
18C 3 medium red frogs
18D small yellow frogs
18E small blue frogs

20A 5 small green frogs
20B 4 small orange frogs
20C 2 medium green frogs
20D small green frogs

21A 5 small green frogs
21B 2 medium green frogs
21C small green frogs
21D medium green frogs

22A small green
22B medium green
22C small blue frogs and small yellow frogs

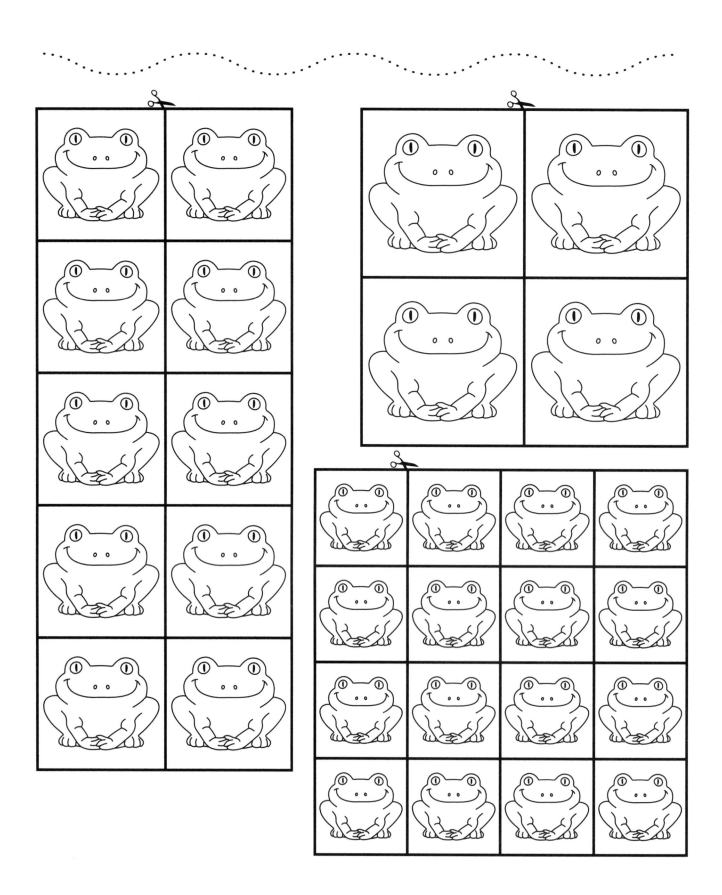

Use small frogs.
Record your work.

Match the frogs.

Sort your frogs by color.
Put each frog where it belongs.

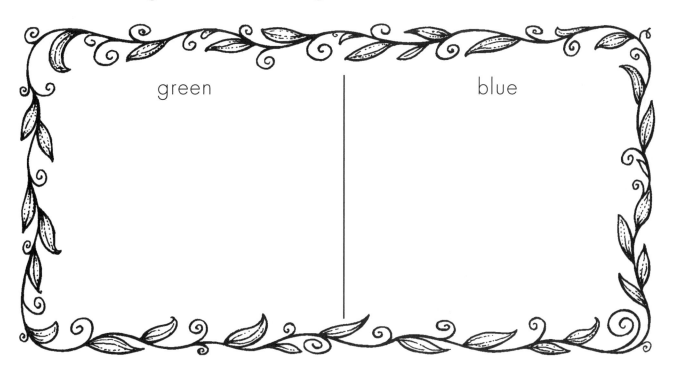

green   blue

A. How many green frogs? _____

B. How many blue frogs? _____

ACTIVITY 2

Use small and
medium frogs.
Record your work.

Name _____

Match the frogs.

Sort your frogs by size.
Put each frog where it belongs.

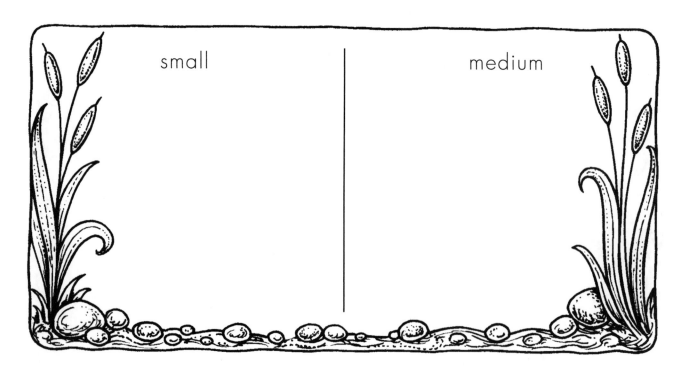

small | medium

A. How many small frogs? _____

B. How many medium frogs? _____

C. Which group has fewer frogs? _____

D. How many fewer frogs? _____

ACTIVITY 3

Use small and
medium frogs.
Record your work.

Name _____

Match the frogs.

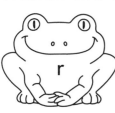

Sort your frogs by color and size.
Put each frog where it belongs.

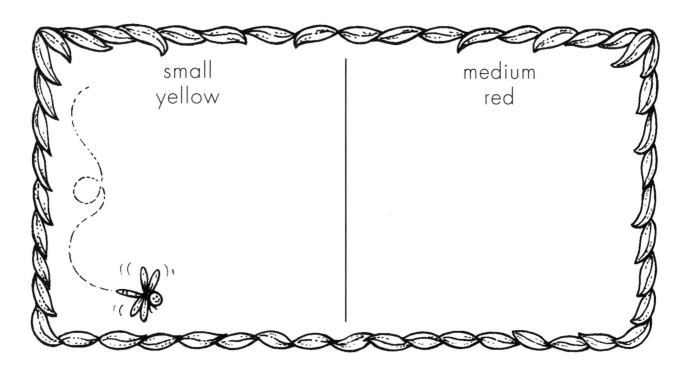

small yellow	medium red

A. How many small yellow frogs? _____

B. How many medium red frogs? _____

C. Which group has more frogs? _____

D. How many more frogs? _____

ACTIVITY 4

Use small and
medium frogs.
Record your work.

Name _____

Match the frogs.

Sort your frogs by color and size.
Put each frog where it belongs.

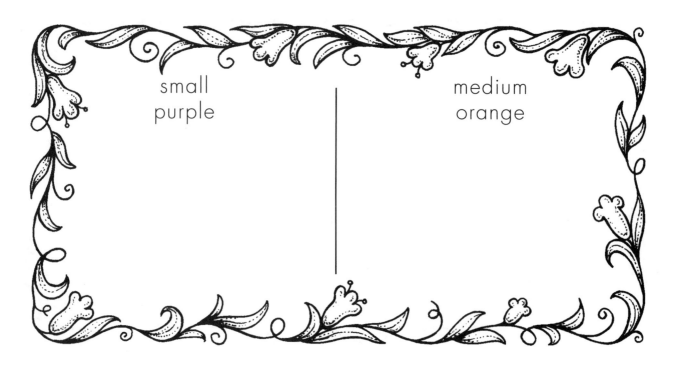

small	medium
purple	orange

A. How many small purple frogs? _____

B. How many medium orange frogs? _____

C. Which group has more frogs? _____

D. How many more frogs? _____

Use small frogs.
Record your work.

Name _____

Match the frogs.

Sort your frogs by color.
Start at the bottom of the graph.
Put each frog on the graph where it belongs.

Color the squares to record.

A. How many
   yellow frogs?_____

B. How many
   orange frogs?_____

C. Which group
   has more frogs?_____

D. How many
   more frogs?_____

Yellow and Orange Frogs

Number of frogs

5

4

3

2

1

Use small frogs.
Record your work.

Name _____

Match the frogs.

Sort your frogs by color.
Start at the bottom of the graph.
Put each frog on the graph where
it belongs.

Color the squares to record.

A. How many
red frogs?_____

B. How many
blue frogs?_____

C. Which group
has fewer frogs?_____

D. How many
fewer frogs?_____

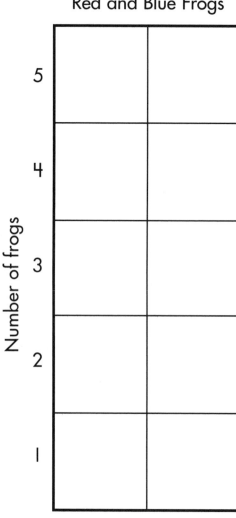

Red and Blue Frogs

Number of frogs

5

4

3

2

1

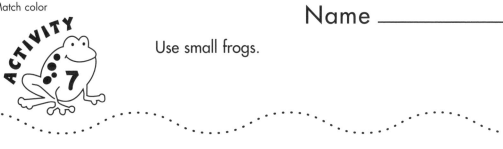

ACTIVITY 7

Use small frogs.

Match the frogs.

Frog Pond

ACTIVITY 8

Use Frog Pond
and small frogs.
Record your work.

Name _____

Match the frogs in Frog Pond.

Sort your frogs by color.
Start at the bottom of the graph.
Put each frog on the graph where it belongs.

Color the graph to record.

A. How many
green frogs?_____

B. How many
yellow frogs?_____

C. Which group
has more frogs?_____

D. How many
more frogs?_____

Frog Pond Frogs

Number of frogs

5

4

3

2

1

g   y

ACTIVITY 9

Use Frog Pond
and small frogs.
Record your work.

Name _____

Match the frogs in Frog Pond.

Sort your frogs by color.
Start at the bottom of the graph.
Put each frog on the graph where it belongs.

Color the graph to record.

A. How many
red frogs? _____

B. How many
blue frogs? _____

C. Which group
has fewer frogs? _____

D. How many
fewer frogs? _____

Frog Pond Frogs

Number of frogs

5

4

3

2

1

r   b

Use Frog Pond
and small frogs.
Record your work.

Name _____

Match the frogs in Frog Pond.

Sort your frogs by color.
Start at the bottom of the graph.
Put each frog on the graph where it belongs.

Color the graph to record.

A. How many
orange frogs?_____

B. How many
purple frogs?_____

C. Which group
has more frogs?_____

D. How many
more frogs?_____

Frog Pond Frogs

Number of frogs

5

4

3

2

1

o   p

ACTIVITY 11

Use small frogs.

Match the frogs.

Frog Park

Use Frog Park
and small frogs.
Record your work.

Name _____

Match the frogs in Frog Park.

Sort your frogs by color.
Start at the bottom of the graph.
Put each frog on the graph where it belongs.

Color the graph to record.

Frog Park Frogs

A. How many
green frogs?_____

B. How many
yellow frogs?_____

C. How many
orange frogs?_____

D. Which group has
the most frogs?_____

E. Which group has
the fewest frogs?_____

Number of frogs

5

4

3

2

1

g   y   o

ACTIVITY 13

Use Frog Park
and small frogs.
Record your work.

Name _____

Match the frogs in Frog Park.

Sort your frogs by color.
Start at the bottom of the graph.
Put each frog on the graph where it belongs.

Color the graph to record.

A. How many
orange frogs?_____

B. How many
purple frogs?_____

C. How many
blue frogs?_____

D. Which group has
the most frogs?_____

E. Which group has
the fewest frogs?_____

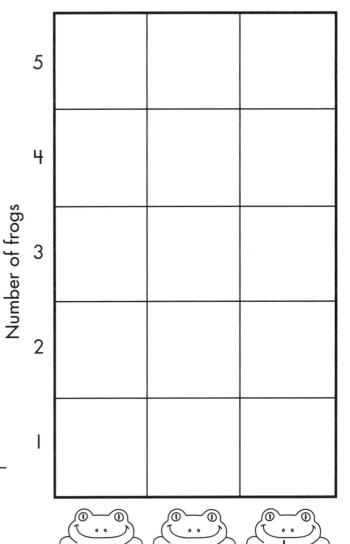

Frog Park Frogs

Number of frogs

5
4
3
2
1

o   p   b

Use Frog Park
and small frogs.
Record your work.

Name _____

Match the frogs in Frog Park.

Sort your frogs by color.
Start at the bottom of the graph.
Put each frog on the graph where it belongs.

Color the graph to record.

Frog Park Frogs

A. How many
blue frogs? _____

B. How many
green frogs? _____

C. How many
purple frogs? _____

D. Which group has
the most frogs? _____

E. Which group has
the fewest frogs? _____

Number of frogs

5

4

3

2

1

b   g   p

Use small and
medium frogs.

Name _____

Match the frogs.

Use Frog House and small and medium frogs. Record your work.

Name _____

Match the frogs in Frog House.
Sort your frogs by color and size.
Start at the left side of the graph.
Put each frog on the graph where it belongs.

Color the graph to record.

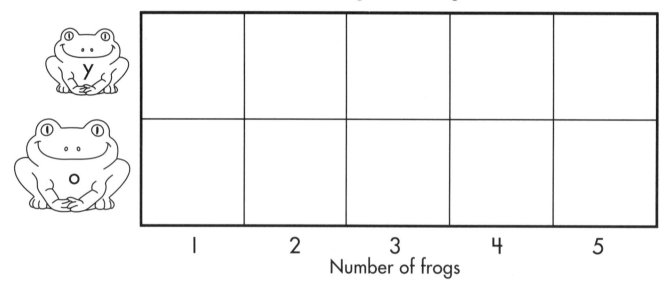

Frog House Frogs

Number of frogs

A. How many small yellow frogs?_____

B. How many medium orange frogs?_____

C. Which group has more frogs?_____

D. How many more frogs?_____

Use Frog House and small and medium frogs. Record your work.

Name _____

Match the frogs in Frog House.
Sort your frogs by color and size.
Start at the left side of the graph.
Put each frog on the graph where it belongs.

Color the graph to record.

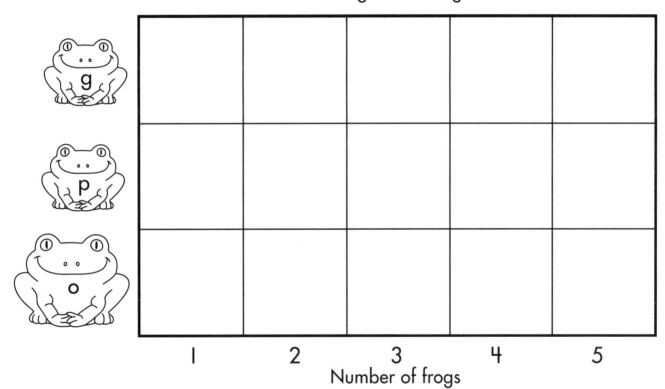

Frog House Frogs

Number of frogs

A. How many small green frogs?_____

B. How many small purple frogs?_____

C. How many medium orange frogs?_____

D. Which group has the most frogs?_____

E. Which group has the fewest frogs?_____

ACTIVITY 18

Use Frog House and small and medium frogs. Record your work.

Name _____

Match the frogs in Frog House.
Sort your frogs by color and size.
Start at the left side of the graph.
Put each frog on the graph where it belongs.

Color the graph to record.

Frog House Frogs

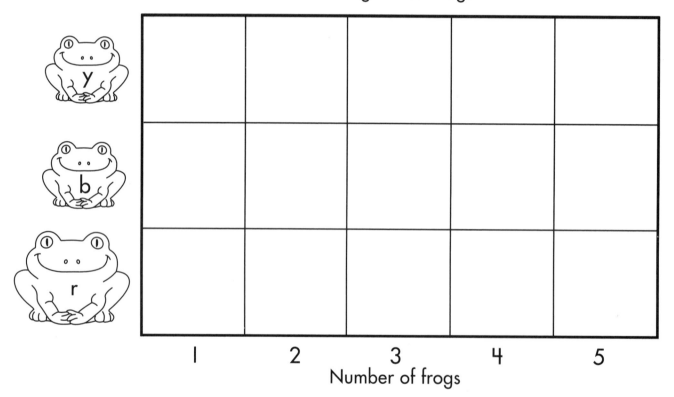

Number of frogs

A. How many small yellow frogs? _____

B. How many small blue frogs? _____

C. How many medium red frogs? _____

D. Which group has the most frogs? _____

E. Which group has the fewest frogs? _____

ACTIVITY 19

Use small and
medium frogs.

Name _____

Match the frogs.

Frog Town

ACTIVITY 20

Use Frog Town and small and medium frogs. Record your work.

Name _____

Match the frogs in Frog Town.
Sort your frogs by color and size.
Start at the left side of the graph.
Put each frog on the graph where it belongs.

Color the graph to record.

Frog Town Frogs

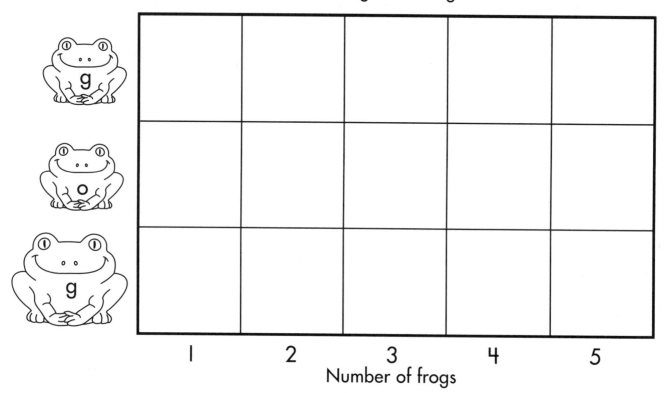

Number of frogs

A. How many small green frogs? _____

B. How many small orange frogs? _____

C. How many medium green frogs? _____

D. Which group has the most frogs? _____

Use Frog Town and small and medium frogs. Record your work.

Name _____

Match, then sort your frogs by color and size.
Color the graph to record.

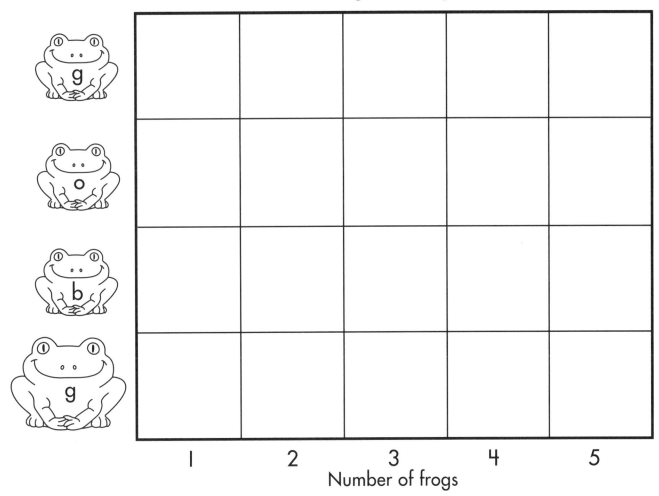

Frog Town Frogs

Number of frogs

A. How many small green frogs?_____

B. How many medium green frogs?_____

C. Which group has the most frogs?_____

D. Which group has the fewest frogs?_____

Use Frog Town and small and medium frogs. Record your work.

Name _____

Match, then sort your frogs by color and size.
Color the graph to record.

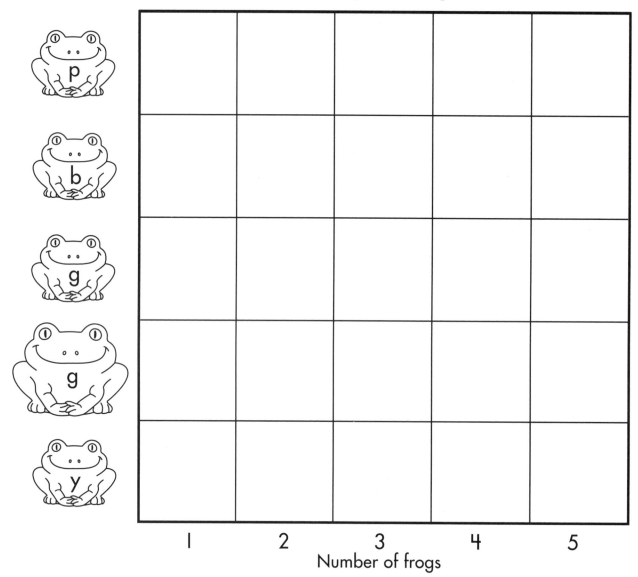

Frog Town Frogs

Number of frogs

A. Which group has the most frogs?_____

B. Which group has the fewest frogs?_____

C. Which groups have the same number of frogs?_____